VALLEY
50690010 ✓ **W9-APN-156**
McGahey, Suzanne.
Winter guard /

VALLEY COMMUNITY LIBRARY
739 RIVER STREET
PECKVILLE, PA 18452
 (570) 489-1765
www.lclshome.org

12/4/07 Direct 19.95

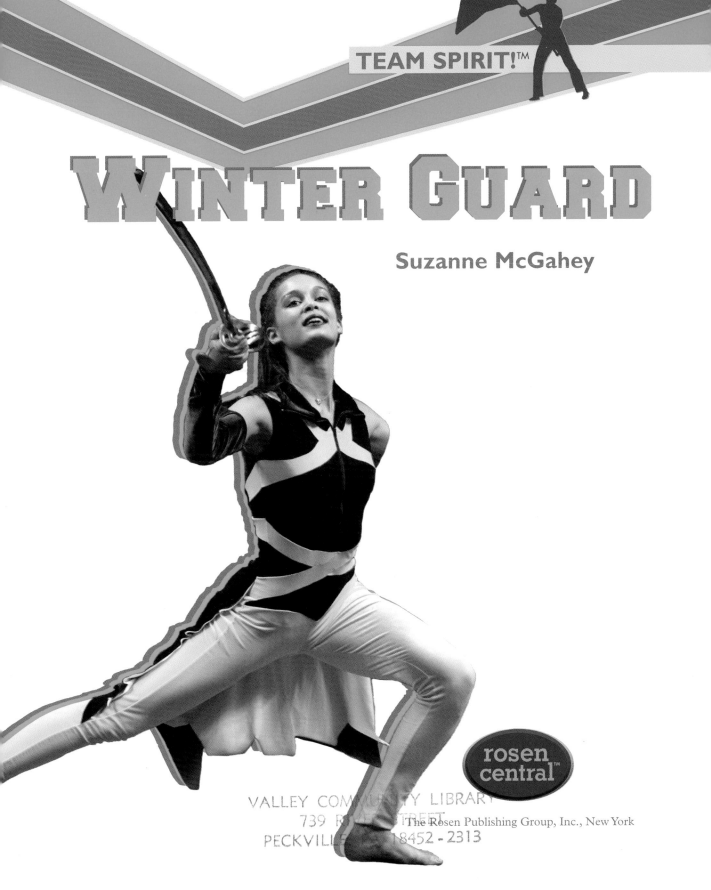

TEAM SPIRIT!™

WINTER GUARD

Suzanne McGahey

rosen
central™

VALLEY COMMUNITY LIBRARY
739 RIVER STREET
PECKVILLE, PA 18452 - 2313

The Rosen Publishing Group, Inc., New York

To my husband, Mark, and my two daughters, Samantha and Zoey. Thank you for supporting me in my endeavors and putting up with my consistent absences on the weekends during my travels.

Published in 2007 by The Rosen Publishing Group, Inc.
29 East 21st Street, New York, NY 10010

Copyright © 2007 by The Rosen Publishing Group, Inc.

First Edition

All rights reserved. No part of this book may be reproduced in any form without permission in writing from the publisher, except by a reviewer.

Library of Congress Cataloging-in-Publication Data

McGahey, Suzanne.
Winter guard/Suzanne McGahey.—1st ed.
    p. cm.—(Team spirit!)
Includes bibliographical references and index.
ISBN 1-4042-0732-5 (lib. bdg.)
1. Winter guards—Juvenile literature.
I. Title. II. Series: Team spirit! (New York, N.Y.)
GV1797.M34 2007
791—dc22

                                                          2006001730

Manufactured in the United States of America

On the cover: Tarpon Springs High School winter guard from Tarpon Springs, Florida, competes in the Scholastic World Finals at the Color Guard World Championships on April 8, 2005.

CONTENTS

THE LURE OF WINTER GUARD

A group of eighth-grade students sat nervously in the high school gym, waiting for their first day of winter guard tryouts. They did not know what to expect. As they waited in the gym, they were told that the winter guard was going to perform its basketball halftime and competition show.

The winter guard entered the gym in a single file, marching in time and setting up for its performance. The newcomers were fascinated by everything from the colorful uniforms to the elaborate display of flags and rifles. They didn't know the song the guard performed to, but most were thinking that this was definitely something that they wanted to do.

Winter guard is one of the fastest-growing activities in the pageantry arts. Colorful uniforms, props, and floor designs are put together to create a five- to eight-minute performance that integrates flags, rifles, sabers, and dance.

For the rest of the week, the new candidates would be taught how to stand, spin, march, and dance, as well as basic flag skills such as angles, carves, spins, and tosses. For some, this would be their first introduction to dance. It would be one of the hardest things some of them had done up to that point, but it seemed like it would be rewarding and fun. The candidates were also shown the routine they were to perform for everyone at the end of the week.

Most of the eighth graders felt that they were the most awkward students in the gym that week, and they worried that they would not make the winter guard. For most, tryouts went better than expected, and to their relief, they made the team. They would then spend the next four years of their lives marching and spinning in the school's winter guard. For many of them, it would be their most enjoyable experience in high school. From there, some would go on to devote much of their lives to winter guard, teaching high school color guard and winter guard units, judging winter guard competitions, and passing on their love of the activity to a new generation.

Winter guard is one of the fastest-growing pageantry activities, which include cheerleading, marching band, indoor percussion ensemble, drum corps, and dance and drill teams. Across the United States, there are about 4,000 winter guard teams, involving approximately 80,000 individuals, that participate in local competitions. Of these, 1,200 winter guard units go on to compete in regional and national championships. The winter guard activity has spread to Europe and

Members of the Miamisburg High School winter guard team from Miamisburg, Ohio, are set to begin their competition program, "Juba." Supporting a theme of stringed instruments, the performers' uniforms have elastic-band attachments that were used throughout the routine.

Asia in recent years. There are now local winter guards and associations in the United Kingdom, the Netherlands, and Japan. These groups spend thousands of dollars to come to the United States and participate in regional and world championships.

CHAPTER 1

The History and Evolution of Winter Guard

Winter guard is essentially a variation on the color guard, which is a flag corps that is associated with a drum corps or marching band. As such, winter guard has its roots in the military tradition of flag ceremonies. Like color guards, winter guards perform elaborate shows that combine the traditional display of flags, sabers, and rifles with dance and military-style drill skills. However, unlike color guards,

A member of the Chino High School winter guard from Chino, California, catches her rifle for a successful completion of a toss.

winter guards perform indoors mostly to recorded rather than live music.

A Military History

Until the late 1800s, military units used flags, sabers, drums, and bugles to signal and position troops, intimidate enemies, stake territorial claims, celebrate conquests, and mourn their dead. Since then, advances in military and communication technologies have relegated these implements and the units that handle them to ceremonial functions.

After World War I, a number of war veterans who belonged to local VFW (Veterans of Foreign Wars) affiliates began forming

This color guard unit of the United States Air Force is responsible for presenting the flag of the nation and state, protected by one rifle on each side. It is from this military history that color guard and winter guard evolved.

marching bands and drum and bugle corps. These musical ensembles were made up of retired war veterans who wanted to continue using the skills they had learned in the military. Many of the VFW drum and bugle corps included a color guard for flag, rifle, and saber presentation.

Soon, other civic organizations, such as the Boys Scouts, and religious organizations began forming their own corps, often with a color guard section. The first drum and bugle corps color guards kept their flags fixed in military-style holsters on the waists of the performers. In time, the guards began using their flags to help interpret the musical style of the drum and bugle corps with simple angles and "slams" (sudden and forceful moves to a forty-five-degree or horizontal angle). Also, the rifle and saber handlers mimicked military drills, displaying their equipment with angles, spins, and simple tosses.

In 1972, Drum Corps International was formed to hold local and national contests for these drum and bugle corps. Today, there are more than 100 such contests. They are held from June to August each year, and they conclude with a national competition during the second week in August. It is from these drum and bugle corps that modern-day color guard and winter guard have evolved.

The Birth of the Winter Guard

Specifically, winter guard began as a spin-off of the Drum Corps International Championships in August 1977, because the drum corps' color guards wanted the opportunity to perform in a separate arena for awards, such as Best Color Guard. At the time, the color guard for each drum corps, consisting of flag, rifle, and saber lines, performed in a separate competition, often in a gymnasium. In the first contest, the competitors performed in the basement of the convention center in Denver, Colorado. They had to perform on a concrete slab and move around large pillars. The first national champions were the Holley Hawks from Holley, New York, who narrowly defeated St. Anthony's Imperiales, also from New York.

Winter Guard International

Until then, there were wide regional differences in guard programs across the country. For example, color guards in Boston emphasized

Members of the New York Holley Hawks pose with their trophies after winning the first-ever color guard national championship in August 1977.

equipment skills, while those in the Midwest emphasized drill. For guards in the West, the emphasis was on dance. It became clear that a national standard was needed, and so Winter Guard International (WGI) was created. Today, WGI is the ruling body that controls most winter guard competitions in the United States. It is a nonprofit organization that promotes music and dance education through winter guard programs.

In October 1977, the founding members of WGI met to establish the rules of competition, the competition schedule (which was moved to the winter months), and a way to crown a national champion. In 1978, the first year of WGI competition, there were fourteen regional contests held across the United States. Today, there are more than twenty WGI regional contests, and one week in April is devoted to a national competition and a world competition.

Avon High School from Avon, Indiana, performs at the Indiana High School Color Guard Association Championships in March 2005. The winter guard team went on to place second in the state championships and fourth in WGI National Championships the following month.

Also, during the first year of winter guard competition, there was only one division of competition, and most of the competing guards were independent units largely made up of college-age participants. In 1980, WGI created the first regional and national championships for high schools. This allowed for a division of competition between the more mature and experienced performers of the independent groups and the younger high school teams, which are known as scholastic groups.

From 1980 to 1985, all high school winter guard teams competed in one class, which is now known as the Scholastic World Class. However, it soon became evident that there was a wide variation in the talent and skill level among high school winter guards. So, in 1985, WGI created the Scholastic A Class for younger teams, allowing them to compete with groups similar to themselves in skill and design level.

After a while, a number of Scholastic A guards had improved their programs so significantly that they began to dominate the competition in that class. In response, WGI created the Scholastic Open Class in 1993 to bridge the gap between Scholastic A and Scholastic World. The dominant Scholastic A guards were then promoted to the new Scholastic Open Class to once again allow for growth and a more balanced competition in the Scholastic A Class. Today, there are six competing winter guard classes. There is a World Class, an Open Class, and an A Class for both scholastic groups and independent groups.

The A Class teams are typically those whose programs are new or whose members and/or instructors are new to the activity. Open Class guards usually have more mature performers with a number of years of experience and have instructors who are more advanced with the choreography. World Class competitions are considered the domain of the elite performers and instructors. These performers and instructors are innovators in the activity and are the model for the other classes.

In addition to Winter Guard International, several companies sponsor and promote winter guard competitions. Marching Auxiliaries is one of them. Based in Texas, this company holds local contests at

Avon High School presents an advanced skill in their Scholastic World program. These performers are required to work together to maintain balance and control, and each group must be perfectly in time with one another.

the middle school and high school levels and hosts training camps throughout the nation during summer and fall. People who are interested in learning the basic skills necessary to participate in winter guard can attend these camps and be taught a number of equipment and dance skills. Marching Auxiliaries also holds eleven regional competitions and a national competition each year.

There are also many local winter guard associations. The local associations comprise high schools and independent teams. They sponsor winter guard competitions from January to late April. Many local contests are held at area high schools, and they are often fund-raisers for the sponsoring school's guard program. These contests typically feature between ten and seventy winter guard units.

By combining equipment moves with dance and drill responsibilities, these cadet winter guard members are demonstrating advanced skills for their age group.

In addition to competitions for the classes established by WGI, local competitions have competitive classes for cadet winter guards. A cadet program features performers who are of elementary- to middle-school age. It is usually associated with the band program at the school. These programs are designed to offer an introduction to the activity, emphasizing the basic equipment and dance skills. Participation in cadet winter guard programs is growing in every local association throughout the nation, as more students are finding that the activity presents new challenges and many rewards. In recent years, cadet winter guard programs have become more sophisticated, as students are learning to spin rifles and sabers at a younger age.

CHAPTER 2

Elements of a Winter Guard Team

Today's winter guard offers opportunities for almost all age groups, and there is usually a winter guard competition in every region of the nation each weekend of the competitive season. There are literally hundreds of winter guard competitions each season. Every Saturday morning from November to April, thousands of winter guard team members arrive at school at sunrise to put in more hours of

Performed by a winter guard member from Choctawhatchee High School in Choctawhatchee, Florida, this heel stretch requires balance, strength, and poise.

rehearsal, hoping to perfect their show and eventually bring home a trophy.

Making the Team

People who wish to join a winter guard unit usually have to participate in a tryout. Most scholastic winter guards provide an information packet (often in the music department), and many post the tryout date and requirements online. The packet typically includes general information about the squad, costs (such as membership fees), rehearsal and performance schedules, parental consent forms, and other requirements. It is important that candidates prepare and submit the required forms on time, and show up to the tryout with a positive attitude and a willingness to commit to the team's schedule.

Each program approaches tryouts differently, but most performers are asked to perform a list of skills in front of a panel of judges and are given a score based on their performance of the needed skills. The try-out process can be somewhat overwhelming for performers who are new to winter guard. Most people who are trying out for a spot on a winter guard for the first time have never touched a piece of equipment, or they may have little, if any, formal dance training. This can be very intimidating for candidates, but what one must remember is that every-one started from scratch at some point and worked through the levels of skill and competition.

The Team

A winter guard team comprises five to thirty members who dance, march, and handle three types of equipment in an elaborate and enter-taining interpretation of a musical work. Typically, the younger winter guard units are divided into three main sections, called lines, based on the three types of equipment: flags, rifles, and sabers. Such divisions are uncommon on the more advanced units, where all team members are usually trained on all three types of equipment.

Most winter guards select a small group of student leaders who have the responsibilities of managing the winter guard in small group rehearsals, dealing with personal issues or problems, and helping to maintain positive attitudes and confidence among the members. These officers are usually the most experienced members of the team. Being a

After spending countless hours together in rehearsals and competitions, most winter guard performers find their best friend sitting right beside them. The common experiences, both good and bad, help to make friendships that will often last a lifetime.

student-leader is a difficult task. He or she must be a friend to his or her peers and must also take on the role of boss during rehearsal and performance times. Fellow students may become resentful of their officers' control, which sometimes strains friendships. However, this is often quickly overcome in the winter guard environment, where teamwork is emphasized.

Of course, the director of the winter guard team has the final say in all matters. The director is responsible for developing the winter guard program, training the team, and deciding what competitions and performance opportunities to pursue. Most winter guard directors work with a staff of other coaches, instructors, and choreographers, who, with the director, make up the design team.

The Winter Guard Program

The typical director will begin brainstorming ideas for his or her winter guard's show months before the competition season begins. Then, in the summer or fall, he or she will begin a series of meetings with the design team to discuss the upcoming performance and competition season. It is during these meetings that major decisions will need to be made: What type of show should the guard perform? What should the stage and floor look like? What costumes will the performers wear? How many members should there be?

Led by the director, the design team writes and stages the winter guard show. This involves deciding what pieces of equipment to use during the show and when to use a piece of equipment or present a dance phrase. This also involves creating the choreography of the program, including equipment, dance, and drill, to present a visual representation of the music. Once the winter guard members have been taught the program, staging involves "cleaning," or fine-tuning, the work and movement. The design of the show is intended to be unique.

The typical design team will spend ten to twelve months creating a show and up to five or six months working on the show with the performers. They teach the work and then try to perfect every move of every performer. The overall goal is to have a team that is properly trained for its competing class and to have everyone achieving the skills at the same level and in the same manner.

Winter guard programs must maintain a minimum amount of equipment time with flags, rifles, or sabers. Class A guards usually spend more time spinning flags than they do handling the rifles or sabers. The weapons are generally considered to be more advanced pieces of equipment, while the flag is the introductory piece of equipment. As guards become more experienced with design and performance, they will begin devoting more time to rifles and sabers. In the Open Class and World Class, it is expected that most, if not all, members will be trained on all three pieces of equipment.

Winter Guard Equipment

The flag is defined as any material fabric to a pole, with a minimum size of eight inches by twelve inches. Because the definition of a flag is relatively broad, designers may choose to use a larger flag for more

Kings High School of Kings Mills, Ohio, presents its 2005 program entitled "Charmed," performed to a selection of Billy Joel songs. The performers demonstrate an excellent understanding of flag skills, combined with dance, to portray a soft and lyrical program.

lyrical songs to create a softer feel and flow, or they may choose to use a brightly colored flag for more aggressive programs.

The look and choreography of the flag design helps to enhance the overall visual ideas of the program. The color and design of the flag give the program its visual effect and is absolutely crucial when designing the show.

While the rifles and sabers do not offer color, they can be used in a way that adds to the style of the program. The rifle or saber can be spun in an aggressive or lyrical (fluid) manner to enhance the style. In winter guard, a rifle is any device constructed to have the appearance of a military rifle. Winter guard rifles today are made of wood with simulated bolts and a leather strap. A saber is a weapon designed to cut, thrust, or slash. A winter guard saber is merely a prop with dull edges that is not meant to be used as a weapon. It has either a curved or straight blade made of wood, plastic, or metal. It must also have a hilt, or handle, and be at least twenty-four inches long.

Although the rifle and saber are based on military equipment, they have been redesigned over time to enhance the vocabulary of winter guard programs. (Within the performing arts, the word vocabulary refers to a system, or collection, of techniques related to the art form.) Flags, rifles, and sabers are tossed from every angle imaginable, and the body is constantly moving underneath or together with the equipment. The catches can happen along any part of the equipment. At one time, the equipment was spun only vertically, appearing flat to the audience. Now, equipment phrases have multiple planes and are much longer in length. A flag phrase may go

Winter guard members must fulfill many responsibilities at one time. They must communicate with the audience, control their equipment and bodies, and interpret the musical soundtrack.

from the vertical plane, to the horizontal plane, and then cut through a 45-degree plane within a matter of only a few musical counts. The outcome is a design that is more visually appealing.

The layering of body and equipment has become increasingly intricate over the past twenty years. At one time, winter guard members performed only one skill—spinning, moving in drill, or dancing—at a time. Now all three elements occur simultaneously, requiring performers and designers to have more training and skill. Performers must understand how the body and equipment work together in a musical phrase to create a truly blended phrase. By the time the equipment and dance skills are taught and mastered, months of preparation and training have gone into the program. The rewards come once the team performs for an appreciative audience.

CHAPTER 3

Winter Guard Training

After months of preparation and tryouts, the hard work really begins. The director and instructors must train the members of the winter guard in all the necessary dance and equipment skills, as well as rehearse the new show. The goal is to have each member perform the skills at the same level and to prepare their bodies for the rigors of the show.

Performers must demonstrate an understanding of equipment and dance technique, as well as accuracy in timing.

Every guard program approaches training in a different way, but they all spend hours on equipment basics and techniques, dance, and movement skills. In some regions, training programs accept children as young as four years old. However, most performers begin their winter guard training in middle school or early high school. The level of competition often depends on age, but it can also depend on whether the guard is scholastic (affiliated with a school) or independent.

In competition, programs are evaluated for their overall quality of design and performance, and each level of competition has different

In a competitive arena, winter guard members must communicate with the audience through their equipment work and by making a personal connection. Winter guards are judged by how well they achieve the skills of their show and how they communicate with the audience.

requirements and skill sets. A cadet winter guard program usually includes basic skills and a show that is relatively simple in design. Most often, cadet programs focus exclusively on flag skills, and dancing and equipment work are usually done one at a time. Cadet members may spin through one musical phrase, move to their staging spot, and then spin or dance once again. Musical soundtracks are often simple, and the choreography is simply meant to visually interpret the music.

As performers and designers grow and mature, they will move on to programs that are more challenging in terms of design and choreography. The A Class show will provide greater performance opportunities as members portray characters or personalities throughout their program. The equipment and dance skills are also more advanced in this class. Performers will spin and dance simultaneously, while fulfilling their drill, or staging, responsibilities. The soundtrack remains relatively simple, with an obvious tempo and an uncomplicated melody.

Once performers and designers are ready to compete at the next level, they must present more complex programs. In the Open Class, performers may be introduced to a conceptual program, one in which they attempt to tell a story or relay a concept. An example may be a show as complex as dealing with the death of a loved one or as simple as portraying the changes of the seasons. The show could involve multiple equipment changes, color changes, and staging changes. Performers may enter and exit the stage to create different textures and moods throughout the program.

In the Open Class, equipment and dance choreography become increasingly complex. Performers may be required to toss and catch their equipment while moving throughout the stage. This layering of body and equipment requires a higher level of training, one in which the performer must understand how the body and equipment work together to create a whole new level of choreography.

The highest class of competition, the World Class, also uses advanced concepts and skills, but the detail and intricacy of the choreography, concept, and staging will be at an even higher level. Equipment and movement phrases are longer, require a new level of skill and training, and will be connected throughout the program. It would not be unusual to see an equipment phrase where the guard begins standing, goes down to the floor, and then comes back up to finish the phrase.

Open Class and World Class performers will also spin the equipment off their bodies, not using their hands, to finish a phrase. For example, they may lie down on the floor, on their backs, and spin the equipment with or around their legs and feet. This requires a whole new level of understanding of how the equipment and body can work together. So, while the cadet performer will spin and then move, the World Class performer will spin, dance, move in drill, portray a character, and relay a message or concept—all at the same time.

Rehearsal

With each level of competition, there comes a different level of training and rehearsal time. In highly competitive programs and divisions, training and rehearsal can go up to thirty or more hours per week. The average for a cadet or A Class program is more likely to be eight to ten

Lifts require dance training in order to prevent injury, as well as an understanding of interdependence. The members being lifted must have strong faith in their teammates and knowledge of balance and control.

hours per week. No matter how many hours per week are devoted to rehearsal, each rehearsal time is divided between honing equipment technique, practicing movement and dance skills, and rehearsing the competitive program.

A typical four-hour winter guard rehearsal usually begins with thirty minutes of stretching to loosen the muscles and prevent injuries. This is followed by a dance technique class, in which the guard members work on basic dance moves, such as kicks, leaps, and pliés (bending at the knees).

Once the basic dance positions are rehearsed, it is time to work on "across the floors," which are dance steps, such as a jazz run, that move the member from one spot on the floor to another. This portion of the rehearsal may run between thirty minutes and one hour.

After the dance section, most winter guards move into their equipment warm-ups, which last from thirty to sixty minutes. It is during this time that members work on the basic flag, rifle, and saber moves that will be integrated into the performance routine.

The rest of the rehearsal will be devoted to learning and perfecting the performance routine. There is usually a small block of time devoted at the end of rehearsal to stretch out once again to avoid muscle cramps, soreness, and injury.

A good program will demonstrate strong levels of training, with each member showing the same level of skill and expression. A well-trained team has members who present all of the dance and equipment skills in exactly the same manner and at the same level of achievement. For example, if a rifle line, consisting of eight members, throws a vertical toss in which the rifle

Demonstrating excellent balance and control, the Bartram Trail High School winter guard team performs extensions and stretches during a practice session at the school. Each member must approach the skills in the same way and achieve them at the same level in order for the routine to be effective.

rotates twice in the air—a skill known as a double—then each member must hold the rifle in the same position, at the same place on their bodies. They must also release the rifles in the same manner, have them spin together in perfect tempo and at the same height, and then catch them in exactly the same way, with their bodies in the same position. The ultimate goal is for each member of the team to have the same approach to the equipment and movement skills, and for everyone to look alike.

VALLEY COMMUNITY LIBRARY
739 RIVER STREET
PECKVILLE, PA 18452 - 2313

Members of the Lealta High School winter guard are pictured with their rifles in midair. Absolute concentration and control are necessary in order for each member to complete the catch successfully.

In addition to the training that takes place on school days, there are also a series of camps that introduce the skills needed for a competition show. The camps typically last one to two weeks and are five to eight hours per day. During the camps, members work on equipment basics, such as angles, spins, carves, hand-to-hand changes, body wraps, tosses, and dancing while spinning the equipment. They also learn new dance and movement skills. These include ballet positions, such as relevé (standing on toes) and tondues (small kicks), various other kicks, and a jazz run.

Memory and Patience

Because nothing is ever written down, team members learn by repetition and memorization. Also, they have to adapt to changes very quickly. When an equipment, dance, or movement phrase is taught, it is simply shown to the members by counts. There is nothing in writing to remind them from one rehearsal to the next what the choreography is. It must be committed to memory. It is also not unusual for multiple versions of a phrase to be taught. Directors may want to see what a drill or staging change looks like, or to rewrite a flag phrase. The winter guard member must adapt to these changes very quickly and remember them for the rest of the season. In some rehearsals, learning must happen at a lightning pace, while in others, hours may be spent fine-tuning one flag or dance phrase. This takes patience and an incredible attention to detail.

Because even the smallest detail must be well-planned and executed, some rehearsals may seem tedious. It is then that the winter guard members must demonstrate their patience and understanding and keep a positive attitude.

Preventing Injuries

Winter guard is a very demanding activity, requiring extensive training in equipment and dance. There may be a number of physical obstacles for a performer to overcome. Because members often begin at the elementary- or middle-school level, their bodies are not quite prepared for the physical stress. It is important that each member receive the proper education and instruction when learning how to perform the dance moves or equipment skills. The threat of injury is always something directors and performers need to be aware of.

THE BULLDOGS: A SPECIAL WINTER GUARD

There are winter guards that are made up of Special Olympics team members or that have a number of members with physical limitations, such as being confined to a wheelchair.

The Bulldogs are a great example of such a team. This team performs at a number of winter guard contests in southern Florida and even performed at Winter Guard International's Grand Championships in Dayton, Ohio, in April 2004. After their performance, they received a standing ovation from a crowd of over 10,000 screaming fans. This appreciation for their efforts and talents is a great payoff for the members of the team. The physical and mental requirements of a winter guard performance can be wonderful therapy for students with physical or mental challenges.

It is extremely important that designers and choreographers understand the physical development of the students they are directing and train them to withstand the strenuous activity. Stress injuries to the knees and ankles are the most common injuries.With proper care and training, most of these injuries can be avoided.

Other types of injuries result from handling the equipment. It is not easy to toss a flag, rifle, or saber into the air and catch it while on the move, so a number of broken bones have occurred over the years. Again, training and physical development are the best ways to avoid such injuries. Physical conditioning, such as stretching, strength training, and proper dance technique, are imperative to avoid injury. The elements of dance technique and equipment basics are most often the only physical training needed for a winter guard performer. To prevent injuries, winter guard instructors must be thorough in their explanation of skills so team members do not take unnecessary risks.

Most injuries arise when team members attempt a skill before they understand the necessary components of the skill. For example, if someone were to throw a rifle or saber without proper training, he or she would risk breaking a hand or finger, or hitting themselves or someone else, when trying to catch it.

Winter guard dance skills can place physical strain on the body, such as stress fractures to feet and legs, as well as ankle sprains and knee strains. Winter guard members who experience such stresses should immediately alert an instructor, so that the injury is properly assessed right away. Most often, recovery from such injuries revolve around RICE (rest, ice, compression, and elevation).

Winter guard members are part of an athletic team and therefore must think of themselves as being in training. Proper diet and nutrition are essential to maintaining energy throughout a long rehearsal or performance. Moreover, winter guard members must always attempt to stay in strong physical condition.

CHAPTER

4

Performance

When you get right down to it, the number one reason people join winter guards is to perform. While competitive performances are the focus of winter guard activity, there are a number of opportunities for winter guards to perform in noncompetitive settings. Because the winter guard season is January through April, a natural setting for a performance is the halftime show at a basketball game.

This photograph is from a 2005 West Carteret High School winter guard show. The costumes, makeup, and choreography were meant to portray the grace and beauty of swans. West Carteret of Morehead, North Carolina, placed sixth in Scholastic A Finals at WGI National Championships in April 2005.

These are great opportunities for winter guards to perform in front of a live audience and to show off their new programs.

Besides winter guard competitions and basketball halftime shows, there are other performance opportunities for winter guard members. Marching Auxiliaries coordinates the performances for a number of college football bowl games, such as the Capital One Bowl, which receives national television coverage. During halftime of the Capital One Bowl of 2000, hundreds of guard members took the field to perform with live musical artists. Television audiences also see guards during the Macy's Thanksgiving Day Parade and the Rose Bowl Parade. Over the course of a winter guard career, performers could potentially entertain tens of thousands of people, perform 100 different times, and feel like they have accomplished an amazing task. Whether your winter guard is winning award after award or not, the thrill of a performance makes all of the hard work during rehearsals well worth the effort. Besides the hours of rehearsal and planning, there are many other things that make a winter guard competition or performance possible.

The guard usually meets hours before its scheduled performance time. Members need time to stretch, warm up, rehearse any last-minute changes, dress, do makeup and hair, load the bus, and arrive at the performance site. Once at the site, the guard goes through two warm-up sessions. The first session is devoted to "body warm-up," during which the team members will stretch out and go over the movement portion of their program. Typically, the body warm-up lasts between ten and fifteen minutes. After this, the winter guard will begin the equipment warm-up, which also lasts ten to fifteen minutes. During this session, the guard goes over the equipment choreography of its program. Once the warm-ups are over, the guard then proceeds to the performance area. The typical winter guard program lasts anywhere from five to eight minutes. Months and months of work go into perfecting those few minutes of performance.

Winter guard shows are held in gymnasiums and arenas, and they take place in an area the size of a basketball court. Many shows are performed on an elaborate stage that can be set up and torn down in a very short time period, often two minutes or less.

Most winter guards will design a vinyl floor the size of a basketball court. This vinyl floor is meant to enhance the look of their show with the use of colors, pictures, or graphics. Along with the floor, winter guards will often use stage flats to define the stage area and add to the visual package. These allow winter guards to create a theatrical setting. Changes can be made offstage, and entrances and exits can be set up for the performers.

A winter guard program is designed to visually interpret the musical track. As such, it has a strong emphasis on dance. The audience may see a lyrical program heavily influenced by classic ballet, followed by a modern dance performance to a rock song. Groups may choose any type of music, so an audience may see and hear everything from the Beatles to Mozart to hip-hop. Some groups choose to tell a story through their music and performance, while others simply interpret the music. It has become commonplace to use dialogue from a popular movie and layer it with music to create a whole new genre of winter guard program. The only limits to what a program may present are those set by the imaginations of the designers and time requirements for legal equipment.

Avon High School's winter guard team portrays pop singer Madonna's many personas and her music from the 1980s to today in their competition routine. The show ranges in feel from soft and lyrical to fast and furious.

Levels of Competition

There are various levels of competition in winter guard. Most local associations follow the guidelines set by Winter Guard International (WGI). Accordingly, they use WGI's score sheets, rules of competition, and competitive class structure. Marching Auxiliaries offers its own levels of competition, complete with scoring system and rules of competition.

An average local show will have levels of competition defined by the classes established by WGI. The younger and less experienced teams perform during the first rounds of competition. Typically, the cadet groups perform first, followed by the A Class winter guards, the Open Class, and then the World Class. Trophies are given to the top three winter guards in each competing class. A show may begin as early as eight in the morning and run until eleven in the evening.

Local winter guard associations begin the season in January and conclude the season with association championships in late March or early April. The typical winter guard association will have approximately fifteen competing shows in a season. Depending on the size of the association and the area covered, there are sometimes multiple shows in one weekend.

Marching Auxiliaries divides its competitions by Team Flag, Team Rife, Winter Guard Show, Small Color Guard Ensemble (fewer than five members), and Outstanding Color Guard Soloists. Trophies are then given to the top three competitors in each class, and jackets are given to the top soloists in each class.

Structure of WGI Championships

Winter Guard International hosts regional competitions and a national competition. All units wishing to participate in the national competition must attend at least one regional competition during the season. WGI regionals are divided into rounds. Each round consists of ten to twelve winter guards in the same competing class. The three highest scorers for each round then go on to participate in the final competition later that weekend. After the top three winter guards from each round are selected, the next six highest scorers will go onto the finals competition. If there are not enough guards in each competing class to divide into rounds, then all groups will compete against one another. The top three to five winter guard teams per class will move onto the finals competition. WGI then awards trophies to the top three teams in each competing class.

For the national competition, there are several rounds of competition for each competing level. Each guard must first perform in a preliminary round, and the top guards in each round will then move onto the semifinals. The top fifteen guards from the semifinal rounds will go on to the finals competition.

Judging

So what are the winter guards judged on? What are the judges looking for? There are five judges for a winter guard competition, and they

Winter guard members are lined up at the WGI National Championships 2005, anxiously awaiting to hear the final results and the presentation of trophies and medals. The award ceremony at the end of competition day is filled with all of the pageantry of the Olympic Games.

award scores in four categories, or captions. The first caption is called general effect. There are two judges in the general effect caption, and both judges sit upstairs in the gymnasium or performance area. These judges evaluate the creativity and originality of the program concept; the imagination, quality, and pacing of the design through equipment, movement, and staging; and the creation of mood through effective use of costumes, props, and set. They also judge the performers' ability to bring the show to life through the successful demonstration of performance skills.

Each general-effect judge has 200 points to award each program. The first 100 points are considered for the design of the show, and the other 100 points are considered for the ability of the performers. In other words, 100 points could be awarded for what the winter guard is performing, and 100 points could be awarded for how the winter guard is performing it.

The second caption, having only one judge, is ensemble analysis. The ensemble-analysis judge gives credit for the quality and depth of the composition and for the design of the equipment, movement, and staging. This judge also considers how well the choreography reflects the musical soundtrack. One hundred points are devoted to the design of the show. Another 100 points are allocated to reward the performers for their technical achievement.

There are two more captions. However, judges for these captions sit downstairs in the gymnasium and look at individual members of the winter guard rather than the whole team. The judge for the equipment caption awards up to 200 points to each guard. There are 100 points possible for the written vocabulary of the equipment book—that is, what they do with the equipment, such as spins and tosses—and there are 100 points possible for the achievement of those skills by the performers. The equipment judge looks to make sure that each member of the winter guard is executing moves at the same time and in the same manner.

judges analyze what the winter guard does with its equipment and compare individuals to see if they are acting in unison. They look for correct angles, timing, and body positioning, as well as the expressive qualities of both the performers and their equipment.

The last caption is movement, or dance technique. Judges for this caption also consider the individual performers. The judge awards up to 100 points for the vocabulary of the movement choreography and up to 100 points for the technical excellence of the performers. Once again, the goal is for each member to achieve the movement skills at the same level and in the same manner. The scores from each judge are then compiled for the total score of the program.

Each competitive class is scored on the same criteria. However, there are different expectations for each class. The cadet winter guard, made up of elementary- and middle-school students, is not evaluated on the same level of technique as that of the more mature performers in the Open Class and World Class.

When the design of the program and the maturity and experience of the performers are higher, expectations are raised. Judging becomes much more critical at the higher competition levels. In the Cadet Class and A Class, the responsibility of the judges is to nurture both the instructor and the performer. Their goal is to educate instructors on how to design a program and how to train the team's members, and to teach members how to perform their show. In the Open Class and World Class, the judges are viewed more as art critics. The goal at this level is to challenge instructors and performers to push for higher goals and expectations.

Even though judges have different standards for each class, the goal is the same: to reward innovative and creative programs, as well as winter guard members who deliver excellent performances.

CHAPTER
5

Winter Guard:
An Art or a Sport?

Because of the physical and mental demands on performers, many people ask: is winter guard a fine art or a sport? The answer is that winter guard is both. Any activity that requires highly trained participants to compete as a team in a highly physical activity for long periods of time can be considered a sport. Winter guard has all the aspects of a sports team, with a few added elements.

A member of the Lealta High School winter guard of San Diego, California, moves her saber through a forty-five-degree position while dancing with finesse.

Winter guard is also creative, beautiful, expressive, lyrical, fun, and artistic. Members must understand musical lines and tempos. They must be actors on a stage, as well as dancers in a musical. Also, they must express the ideas of the program, or music, through their equipment and choreography.

The one element of team sports that winter guard does not have is the requirement for being on the defensive. Winter guards are always on the offensive. Winter guard teams compete against a standard instead of directly against another team, much like a gymnast or diver. All a winter guard team can do is perform its show to the best of its ability and leave the rest to the judges. It is then those five people who will rate and rank each of the winter guard programs to decide the winner.

Competition is an important aspect of any sport, and winter guard has its top competitors and competitions. Its various regional and national trophies are as highly regarded among winter guard enthusiasts as are the Lombardi Trophy among football fans and the Stanley Cup in professional hockey. The week-long National Championship held by WGI is considered to be the Super Bowl of winter guard. More than 4,000 teams participate each year for top honors in their competitive classes.

Because of its combination of sports and artistic elements, winter guard is often referred to as "the sport of the arts." Today's winter guard members are athletes, actors, and experts with their equipment.

A Lifetime of Benefits

The thrill of performing in front of an audience that appreciates your hard work and achievement is probably the most rewarding aspect of winter guard, but there are many others. Members often make friendships that will last a lifetime, earn scholarships, or find their career path. However, the number one answer that winter guard

Most competitive winter guard units dream of winning national championships. However, performing for an appreciative audience provides the greatest reward of all.

members give for their love of the activity is the excitement of performing for an audience of cheering fans.

The typical winter guard audience member is very educated in the activity and appreciative of a great performance. Members will hear thunderous applause after a long equipment phrase or completion of a difficult toss and catch. You may receive a standing ovation during or after your show. For winter guard members, few feelings rival the one they get coming away from the performance knowing they gave it their all.

"There is no better feeling than performing in front of a large crowd, especially when you have a great performance," says Megan Inselmann, assistant director of the Flower Mound High School winter guard, of which she was a member. "Winter guard is different from any other sport or activity because it is a combination of so many things, such as athletic ability, dancing of all forms, theater, and sometimes even gymnastics. Winter guard is so diverse. No two guards are the same."

Winter Guard Scholarships

Along with the thrill of performance come other benefits, some of which are financial. Local winter guard associations, along with WGI, offer scholarships to participants who are graduating, or "aging out." WGI offers approximately $200,000 in scholarships each year to between fifteen and twenty participants. These scholarships will then be applied to the cost of college or higher levels of education. Local associations offer scholarships, ranging from $100 to $1,000, to graduating partic- ipants, based on need and academic excellence.

A Career in the Winter Guard

After dedicating years to the winter guard activity, there comes a time when members either graduate from high school or "age out" and must retire their equipment and dance shoes. Winter guard members are allowed to participate on independent teams until they reach the age of twenty-two in the A Class and Open Class. However, in the Independent World Class, there are no age limits. Members may march as long as they wish. In order to participate on a scholastic team, each member must be a current member of the school he or she is representing.

Once members retire as performers, a number of them will become directors or instructors of their own winter guard teams. Once the activity "gets in your blood," it's hard to give it up. Being the director of a winter guard team requires dedication and a love for the activity. The best education for becoming a director or instructor is one's experience as a member of a winter guard team. There is no formal certification for a coach. However, a strong background in dance and equipment skills is a must.

Team members will walk away from their experiences with fond memories, strong friendships, and a sense of what it takes to be a member of a team. The winter guard activity is not about the individual, but the team. It is for this reason that most winter guard directors and instructors are among the ranks of former members and people with education backgrounds. Some are teachers at their high schools, and others own their own dance studios. Some are in the corporate world and direct a winter guard team as their second career. While the path to directing a winter guard may vary, directors and instructors love to work with kids and love the activity of winter guard.

Life Lessons

Being part of a winter guard team helps students develop skills that they will use for the rest of their lives. Participants will understand what it means to truly commit their time and effort to something. It is important to understand the role each member plays when being part of a team. If one person is missing in an equipment or movement phrase, then the intention of the choreography is not clear, and the whole team is penalized.

Winter guard also teaches students about the importance of confidence, time management, positive attitudes, leadership, learning skills, and patience. When entering into the workplace and family life, these life skills will be essential to professional and personal success. The working parent must have the ability to multitask and understand the importance of time management. Participating in a winter guard program provides experience in time management at an early age.

With nights and weekends being consumed with winter guard activities, team members must find time to spend with their families and friends, complete their homework assignments for school, and spend time just being kids. The ability to prioritize tasks and manage time is absolutely essential to success in winter guard as well as life. Corporate executives are also looking for people who can exhibit a strong aptitude for learning and leadership.

Winter guard teaches its members the importance of attitude through rehearsals and performances. The members of the audience don't want to

A member of Pride of Cincinnati emotes as he waves his flag during the winter guard's competitive routine. Using a musical book that included the dialogue of comedians such as Jerry Seinfeld and Margaret Cho, the team was crowned WGI's Independent Gold Medalist in 2005.

see a winter guard performer who is unhappy with what he or she is performing. They want to see a bright, enthusiastic performer who steals the stage and captivates them for the entire performance. Nor can winter guard members approach rehearsal time with a negative attitude. If they do, they will not see many rewards for their efforts.

Winter guard members who are dedicated and enthusiastic are often rewarded for their efforts through successful performances and appreciative crowd response. This helps to build self-confidence. Confidence comes from mastering an equipment phrase that first seemed impossible, completing a dance phrase well from beginning to end, or by leading the team onto the floor for a wonderful performance. A winter guard member may begin in elementary school as a shy, undeveloped performer, but after years of practice and dedication, he or she will emerge as a strong leader, confident performer, and well-rounded individual.

The ability to lead a group of peers is an important quality of a winter guard officer. Every student leader takes away the invaluable experience of leading a team and can apply that to his or her job and life to become a much more successful person. So, while winter guard emphasizes equipment and dance skills, there are many skills that can be learned and applied throughout a lifetime.

An Enduring Passion

Most winter guard members look back on their time spent at rehearsals, at competitions, and with their friends with fond memories. They can recall big portions of their favorite shows and tell great stories about their best performances. The stories usually revolve around a funny thing that happened at practice, or even how they broke their thumb, but they always bring back a great time in the life of the performer.

Once members graduate and go on to have their own families, many pass on their love of the activity to their children. They do this by taking them to contests, showing them old tapes of Mommy or Daddy during a performance, and exposing them to the skills of equipment and dance technique.

So, for the first-time performer or for the person who is trying out for his or her first winter guard team, there are a million experiences that lie ahead. The excitement of learning a new equipment phrase,

Leigh High School of San Jose, California, makes an impressive debut in a winter guard competition with a dazzling show entitled "Loves Me . . . Loves Me Not . . ." The routine, which includes mock roses in addition to traditional winter guard equipment, will make the team a Scholastic World Class finalist in the Winter Guard International Championships in 2005.

the hours spent at rehearsal, the long-lasting friendships, and the thrill of performing in front of an appreciative audience are all things to be remembered fondly once the winter guard experience is over. For most, it is not about winning every competition, it's about the experiences that are accumulated over time.

Glossary

cadet winter guard A winter guard made up of elementary- and middle-school students.

drill The movement of winter guard performers around the floor, either moving in tempo or free-form.

ensemble analysis A judging caption that rewards the design and performance of the winter guard show.

equipment phrase A musical phrase completed on one of the three pieces of equipment. Usually eight to twenty-four counts in length.

flats Standardized units used together to construct theater sets.

general effect A judging caption that rewards the creativity and effectiveness of the winter guard program.

independent winter guard A winter guard that is not affiliated with a particular school.

layering Performing an equipment phrase and dance phrase simultaneously.

movement A dance or drill sequence.

plane The line or area that the equipment or movement phrase travels through, such as a vertical, horizontal, or forty-five-degree plane.

saber A handheld weapon that is designed for cutting, thrusting, or slashing an enemy. In winter guard, it is a prop that has either a curved blade or a straight blade, which may be constructed of wood, plastic, metal, or any other suitable material.

scholastic winter guard A winter guard whose members attend the same school.

staging The placing of winter guard members on the floor to create certain effects, such as lines, blocks, or other forms.

For More Information

Winter Guard International
WGI Sport of the Arts
7755 Pargon Road, Suite 104
Dayton, OH 45459
(937) 434-7100
Web site: http://www.wgi.org

Web Sites

Due to the changing nature of Internet links, the Rosen Publishing Group, Inc., has developed an online list of Web sites related to the subject of this book. This site is updated regularly. Please use this link to access the list:

http://www.rosenlinks.com/team/wigu

For Further Reading

Coachman, Frank. *Marching Bands*. New York, NY: The Rosen Publishing Group, 2007.

Sloan, Karyn. *Techniques of Color Guard* (Let's Go Team: Cheer, Dance, March). Broomall, PA: Mason Crest Publishers, 2003.

Usilton, Terry. *Color Guard Competition* (Let's Go Team: Cheer, Dance, March). Broomall, PA: Mason Crest Publishers, 2003.

Bibliography

Marching Auxiliaries. Various articles. Retrieved September 2005 (http://www.maux.com).

Wikipedia.com. "Color Guard." Retrieved September 2005 (http://en.wikipedia.org/wiki/Color_guard).

Winter Guard International. "History of WGI." Retrieved September 2005 (http://www.wgi.org/about/general.php).

Winter Guard International. "Welcome to the World of WGI." Retrieved September 2005 (http://www.wgi.org/about/general.php).

Index

About the Author

Suzanne McGahey is currently in her fourth year as the color guard and winter guard director at Keller High School in Keller, Texas. She is working with WGI for the fifth competition season as an equipment judge. McGahey resides in North Richland Hills, Texas, with her husband, Mark, and two daughters, Samantha and Zoey.

Series Consultant: Susan Epstein

Photo Credits

Cover, title page, pp. 9, 18, 23, 25, 36, 39, 40, 48, 50, 57 Winter Guard International; pp. 5, 16, 27 Bateman Photography; pp. 7, 8, 13, 15, 31, 43, 46 Avon High School; p. 10 © Bob Daemmrich; p. 12 Holley Hawks; pp. 17, 20, 26, 34, 51 Lealta Winter Guard; pp. 28, 33, 53 Bartram Trial High School; p. 59 Collage Winter Guard.

Designer: Gene Mollica; Editor: Wayne Anderson; Photo Researcher: Marty Levick